THE POWER OF VULNERABILITY

THE POWER OF VULNERABILITY

Embracing Authenticity and Courage

ELARA PHOENIX

QuillQuest Publishers

CONTENTS

CHAPTER 1

Introduction

In a culture that views vulnerability as a weakness, showcasing an authentic display of courage takes real strength. To be genuine and authentic, of course, usually involves at least a little risk and discomfort; in other words, the willingness to be vulnerable. In this guide, you will discover a range of advice and self-help on embracing your vulnerabilities and using them to create a more fulfilling, more thoughtful life!

So mustering up the courage to allow yourself to be more vulnerable is an act of bravery, one that can provide an incredible amount of value to every aspect of your life. There are many stories in these pages from our contributors about how they've benefited from incorporating greater vulnerability into their way of being. Some saw vast improvements in their physical health after letting themselves be unguardedly open; others encountered more success than ever before in their respective careers. Finding love and fulfillment, both personal and professionally, seems infinitely easier once you begin to trust in the unadorned plan of vulnerability. But there are, naturally, some anvil-sized flip-sides to this kind of openness. Vulnerability can, and will, cause pain, and unfortunately, that's not the only side effect. Inevitably, it will also make you far more sensitive, meaning the emotional upturns and downturns will become more pronounced as your awareness becomes more encompassing. Acceptable losses, we'd say, but losses all the same.

CHAPTER 2

Understanding Vulnerability

Moreover, vulnerability is at the core of human connection and caring. Brown posits that when we shield ourselves from vulnerability, we are also closing ourselves off from meaningful relations with others. She continually offers encouragement to her readers throughout the discussion, reiterating the idea that vulnerability is intertwined with the essence of the human experience. Right now, this might feel scary. Of course, this fear is one of the reasons we flee from vulnerability in the first place. Vulnerability requires courage. Vulnerability implies taking risks. Vulnerability is bringing our true selves to a situation while knowing it is possible that we could be rejected. Vulnerability promises that we will not allow any future hurt to prevent us from living as whole-hearted people today. Vulnerability means that we act with courage.

Vulnerability exists in a variety of forms. Brown makes the distinction between situational vulnerability and dispositional vulnerability. Situational vulnerability is exemplified by unique life occurrences, such as sharing and having to express love for someone, getting laid off at work, or facing possible negative consequences. Dispositional vulnerability, however, is symbolic of personal control and choice in relation to courage and action. It is being open and reliant rather than closed through and in spite of fear. These two vulnerability patterns are drastically different, but Brown argues that dispositional vulnerability is ultimate and fundamental to the human experience.

Vulnerability is a term that few people like to embrace. In layman's terms, it sounds like it could only ever be associated with something inherently negative. Brené Brown, however, offers a rather different definition. According to Brown, vulnerability is an emotion that we inherently feel when we are exposed and uncertain. Despite its negative association, vulnerability is crucial and fundamental to human connection.

Defining Vulnerability

Recognizing our vulnerability can cause us to take on a number of attitudes; it can leave us feeling fraught. For instance, sometimes vulnerability is thought of as a type of weakness, allowing us to be assaulted or to cheat or to have something unspeakable revealed about ourselves, although in the technical sense, weakness is the absence of power. When we say, "I believe revealing my feelings to this person would allow me to hand them a gun while loading it," we are referring to vulnerability as weakness. Another way this may be depicted is as fragility, i.e. something that can be lost as in, "I would like to show you my greatest weakness, but I might fall apart as I'm trying to show you." Sometimes people who express the fact that they are vulnerable actually know what their drawbacks are, and by sharing them they can finally embellish the truth or "airbrush the facts". We can also recognize vulnerability as insecurity, although Liz Gilbert concedes that feeling insecure about ourselves has a slightly clever twist worthy of respect. Vulnerability is insecurity when we don't need to feel that way. For example, saying to someone, "Do you like my dress? I'm not sure if it's right."

Essentially, people's stories suggest that vulnerability is uncertainty, risk, and emotional exposure, not knowing what will happen or exactly how a situation will turn out. To let people know you appreciate advantages, some create a type of airbrushed version of society, i.e., compose just enough to make it appear that I am appropriately open. However, what's generally realized is that the lifetime we stay unassured, willing to risk, and emotionally exposed, that is what makes us vulnerable.

Types of Vulnerability

Areas such as marketing, administration, and communication work strongly with vulnerability. In exposing himself, the human being becomes the object of critical and discriminatory looks, and in this scenario, people want protection in sought-for qualities such as fear of losing their jobs, affecting their careers. It is considered constructively positive to always be seeing new opportunities to take on new roles in decision making. It is correct to say that taking risks requires knowledge and careful behavior. In doing so, one can suffer from the threat of exposing themselves to considering mistakes to balance and make responsible decisions. Mistakes are not allowed, society be it being extraordinarily judgmental. While some organizational strategies and practices are created and maintain their strength almost instinctively, decision-making specialists like managers, need to seriously attend combined tasks (Hamel, 2007).

Baby vulnerability marries dependence, while human vulnerability includes death, affection, love, loss, betrayal, and violence. The death that renders humans vulnerable has always been in men's daily conversations, creating chaos from birth and affecting society. Vulnerability became part of the topics of theories of organization and administration, also being placed on management's "agenda".

Feminine authors were instrumental in transforming emotions related to vulnerability into one of the paradigm-shifting themes in administration. Hamel (2007, p. 221) says that nowadays in organizations there are no survivors; people have to be new and reinvent themselves every day to "succeed, let alone survive."

CHAPTER 3

The Benefits of Vulnerability

Being vulnerable is not simply about waiting for unpleasant sensations and emotions to go away – it is about developing strength and resilience in the face of difficulty. When we give ourselves the courage to feel uneasy realities, problems, unpleasant truths, and failures, we can become more capable of coping with adversity, more resistant, and more grounded in the reality of our experiences. This is a mental sturdiness that encourages us to respond productively to life's downs. Vulnerability, if treated with bravery and compassion by ourselves and others, can also help us build stronger connections. When we open up to others about who we are, including our dreams, aspirations, values, and coping mechanisms, we have the ability to create deep, lasting relationships. Such a high level of intimacy is only achievable when individuals express their real feelings and views.

Vulnerability is usually painted in a negative light: it can result in pain, rejection, and various other unpleasant emotions. As a result, we often perceive it as a weakness rather than embracing it as a powerful tool for our benefit. When we change our perspective and start to see vulnerability as an opportunity to grow in a range of areas, we can embrace it for the positive change it can give us. Many acknowledge that the recovery process can make us stronger and wiser, but only some perceive that vulnerability can also result in further personal growth and development. As we encounter our fears and allow ourselves to feel vulnerable in the face of them, we can begin to develop courage, which in turn enables us to set and achieve a variety of different goals for ourselves. This helps us to recognize our potential and increase our confidence in our ability to act.

Personal Growth and Resilience

The vulnerability and resilience (VR) process triggers a paradigm shift in which being vulnerable is transformed from a position of weakness into a position of strength and possibility. Instead of being a toxic conspiracy from our past, our vulnerability can be seen as our main methodology for healing and self-growth. Do we need outer courage to make changes in our lives? No, inner courage is enough because once accessed and put to work, it contains the energy for everything we might consider a better future. There's a kind of structure within this vulnerability-courage bond. Vulnerability breaks us open, softens us, yet it becomes a source of strength, resilience, and healing. It also becomes the pathway to mental, emotional, and behavioral transformation, a runway leading to empowerment.

While the prevailing belief is that vulnerability equals weakness, open-minded research has found quite the opposite: our vulnerability does not make us weak, but it helps us grow and reach beyond belief. Notably, our vulnerability often goes hand in hand with personal growth, resilience, and increased adaptability. Psychological research into resilience has revealed that individuals who practice vulnerability and resilience do not just survive a threatening experience. They find ways of changing how they perceive themselves and the world around them. Their actions down-regulated the intensity of 'fight and flight' mechanisms, allowing them to make a plan of action for themselves calmly and rationally.

Building Stronger Relationships

Moving into a community, embracing vulnerability means that we are inviting others into a relationship with not just the best, curated version of ourselves but with all the warts and shame that we carry inside. In Return to Earth, Daniel MacKenzie invites us to see that wrapping ourselves in protective environments isn't just detrimental to us, but to other people as well. He observes "our physical environment is a great teacher. It clearly shows to me that nobody thrives in antiseptic isolation—nobody." In a world where most people are "calibrating their level of wealth by how much they can have others leave them alone," perhaps willing vulnerability could point to alternatives and, in fact, lead to new worlds. If, as Daniel Quinn suggests, the real power structures in our cultures are determined not by the size of our military budgets but by "the size of our fictions," then the fiction of overcoming our shameful vulnerability (personally, not collectively), could be the very thing holding us back from love, power, and yes, even a personal but very different kind of immortality.

When done willingly, collective vulnerability becomes an invitation to trust and intimacy. As shame researcher Brené Brown acknowledges, "Vulnerability is the core of all emotions and feelings. To feel is to be vulnerable. To believe vulnerability is weakness is to believe that feeling is weakness. To foreclose on our emotional life out of a fear that the costs will be too high is to walk away from the very thing that gives purpose and meaning to living." The protection of our interior lives encased in our physical bodies keeps others distantly defined "others," instead of intimate friends. And greatest of all these connections are those that can move past the definitions of "family" or "blood," to become something even greater because of the relationship you've chosen, not the one you were given.

CHAPTER 4

The Intersection of Vulnerability and Courage

However, despite appearing on opposite ends of the spectrum, vulnerability and courage do intersect. This is because both qualities rely on the presence of the other. It is impossible to be and act with complete courage without first examining and embracing the extent of vulnerability. This requires accepting that vulnerability is a cornerstone for effective and decisive action. Contrary to the popular interpretation of the two traits as confrontational opposites, when linked together, courage springs from the acceptance of vulnerability. Vulnerability, then, fuels courage. Personal growth and empowerment are direct byproducts of integration between the two. Despite their differences, vulnerability and courage exert profound influence on people's choices and behaviors and go hand-in-hand to govern their actions.

At first glance, vulnerability and courage may seem like opposing qualities. At the heart of vulnerability is an acknowledgment and acceptance of deeply personal failures or weaknesses. Coupled with a loss of control, these admissions produce a feeling of exposure intertwined with emotional risk. On the other hand, courage conjures images of overcoming fear, dismantling personal obstacles, and gaining mastery over one's experiences. Inherently confident, courageous people push onward through adversity, undeterred and unlikely to reveal fear or doubt.

CHAPTER 5

Practical Strategies for Cultivating Vulnerability

1. Cultivate self-awareness and self-love: "Making a commitment to self-awareness and introspection is important because it creates self-love." 2. Use empowering language: "Empower yourself further by using the phrase 'I am making a commitment.' This may seem like a subtle shift, but it is powerful in its ability to add another layer of integrity to this device." So, for instance, "I'd like to higher my energy" becomes "I am making a commitment to raise my energy." 3. Establish boundaries: "The fourth way to cultivate and empower vulnerability is to establish and honor your boundaries," Christine tells us. "Be aware and be honest with yourself about how much energy/love/comfort/favor you are willing and able to give/time, money, a portion of yourself etc. to others." Encouraging people to dedicate weekly time for reflection is good, Christine says, because "these checks help empower us, remind us of our vulnerable power, and to surrender when we cannot control the outcome of our environment or the

needs of others." As we practice these five steps, we do in fact surrender the need to control everything, in particular others, to the universe, to a higher power-vector-point, to love. We begin to trust that we are seen and loved for who we are, vulnerable, soft-hearted, and big-balled.

According to Angela, whole-hearted people value vulnerability, connection, and creativity. What about the people who asked her to define vulnerability as having "massive balls and calling it vulner-ability"? Though that may be bravado and chauvinism, if we strip everything away, the guy was saying that to be truly happy, he had to take his armor off, to be vulnerable, to let himself be seen. To have massive balls is to be all in, to be all about, to have given all the armor up. Here are some steps you can take to cultivate true vulnerability, that is, to be courageous and to show up and be seen when you cannot control the outcome.

Self-Reflection and Awareness

One of the first steps in being vulnerable is writing out our challenges, whether they be those small daily annoyances or a lingering heavy heart feeling. Ever notice when you start to add pen or pencil to paper, things begin to shift and release? I encourage everyone to take 5 minutes, open a blank Word document or grab a piece of paper, and start to get raw. Share your fears, blockages, and everything you currently do not feel comfortable sharing. This simple act of writing down our life circumstances increases our awareness and begins to set the stage for vulnerability and courage. Each question that is asked invites us to celebrate a piece of ourselves. Imagine if we strengthened the muscle of courage by offering ourselves a chance to release and take notice of the vastness of our resilience and vulnerable voices.

Investing time in self-reflection is a fundamental piece in strengthening our vulnerability muscles because it can increase self-awareness and promote a mindful presence that paves the way for emotional openness. Brené Brown, a research professor whose thoughtful work surrounds shame, courage, and vulnerability, mentions in her 2010 "Ted Talk" that "vulnerability is our most accurate measurement of courage." When we invest time in self-awareness, we start to see our blind spots, limiting beliefs, and even our potential. We can be vulnerable at any age or stage with the right amount of courage. Start to get real with yourself and others. Be authentic. Embrace your quirks, and most importantly – realize that you matter and your story is important in the grand scheme.

Setting Boundaries

It's really important to me to discuss the necessity of setting boundaries. In fact, setting boundaries is a key method of honeymooning, which we'll discuss in section People often hate the thought of setting boundaries with others because they are tied to cultural expectations that women should always be selfless and giving and never deny others their full time and attention because then you're being stingy and selfish. People have often been called names or shunted out of social circles because they voiced discomfort with the actions of group members. This isn't to say that one single rejection means that vulnerability was traded for shame.

Sometimes, it seems that people are really utilizing vulnerability and authenticity in a manipulative way. Some people believe that we should always be able to be vulnerable with others because they're supposed to be figures of authority and compassion in our lives. But if people aren't careful about sharing in the right amounts with the right people who give it back to them, they could be setting themselves up for a lot of hurt. And then they could be soured to the idea of vulnerability and authenticity with others, even though the source of the pain wasn't the act of sharing, but the specific situation when and how they shared.

Overcoming Barriers to Vulnerability

One of the things Brown notes is that this fear of vulnerability and the shame it leads to results from a number of fears and tendencies: the fear of being rejected, the tendency to reject ourselves or criticize ourselves before we can be rejected by others, and finally the fear of reaching out only to have no one reach back. Vulnerability, she explains, becomes also challenging because society often pressures individuals to stop being genuine or accepting of themselves by imposing particular standards and values; for example, as evident in advertisements or the increasing emphasis on physical appearances and complying with societal standards of beauty and health. Given the problematic and often negative nature of the vulnerability Brown details, is it not surprising that vulnerability is hard for very few to embrace as part of one's own being. There are more unaware of it without doubts.

One of the reasons why we spend most of our lives seeking to become part of and connect with people is that this is a deep part of our being, a biological predisposition. Yet, many of us find it hard to accept, embody, or express the essence of vulnerability within us. Brené Brown, a research professor at the University of Houston Graduate College of Social Work, has been studying vulnerability for over ten years and acknowledges that most people cringe at the word. According to Brown, we usually see vulnerability in society as a weakness, rather than what it truly is: the foundation for connection and courage. Hiding our authentic selves or avoiding connection, she explains, to give the impression that we exist, belong, and are worthy of being appreciated and loved are at the heart of shame.

Fear of Rejection

Bowlby on attachment theory suggests that rejection is experienced in individuals in much the same way as it was for our ancestors. We are much more likely to survive and reproduce if we fit in, likability connects to protection. Therefore, our attachment strategy of trying to fit in has developed through evolution. However, if we have a fear of rejection (stemming from experiences of actual rejection or perceived potential rejection) and criticize ourselves in response to these feelings, the experience of experiencing fear of standing out is greater. Our feelings of shame intensify our distress when facing the possibility of rejection. Brown writes that in her research, many of her participants would try and protect themselves from the fear of rejection by rather pretending that the potential source of rejection does not matter to them. They would withdraw or pretend that they did not care about gaining acceptance. Others would pretend to be the person they thought would be accepted (manipulating the acceptance they receive), rather than share their true version. As we see, our fear of rejection keeps us stuck in a negative self-caring loop. We want to be seen and embraced for our true selves, and yet we fear the exposure of our true selves as it then opens up the possibility of disconnection.

Many people fear exposing their real self to the world in a vulnerable way because of a fear of rejection. However, when we examine this fear more closely, we would see that it stems from a fear of being deemed unworthy, or not enough, to be accepted. What people are really fearing is that their true self, imperfections and all, are unworthy or not enough to be accepted. As we discussed in Part One of this work, esteem is about worth; true belonging is not possible unless we believe ourselves to be worthy. This fear of being deemed unworthy if we show our true selves is tied to a root of the fear of disconnection. When we give up fitting in (pretending or hiding) – the opposite strategy from true belonging – we are risking the possibility of rejection. We could be pushing away the conformity that could possibly give us a false belonging, in hopes of finding true belonging. This is when the ease gets harder and the discomfort requires courage. In order to be accepting of our vulnerabilities and work on developing the necessary courage to expose them, we need to confront our fear of rejection.

Societal Expectations

Society's aversion to sharing our true selves runs so deep we've invented systemic structure to separate public and private life. In essence, time is divided into two equal categories: time you can express vulnerability and honesty with those close to you and time you must suppress, lie about, ignore, or alter your experiences. We call that second, longer part professional and it's a must to be taken seriously, move upward and create value. The worst part? This is deeply unhealthy. Keeping these two lives completely separate can wreak havoc on the body, the emotions, as well as the psyche. In order to be healthy, we must not be politically correct, we must be authentic. And in true form, we must even reveal our political incorrectness and let that be seen, too. For in authenticity, true healing can begin. How do you feel about vulnerability? Are you afraid or excited when you hear the prospect of being more open about your authentic self?

However, vulnerability can expose us to societal prejudices and stereotypes associated with being weak and "less than." We often comment on societal problems like emotional suppression, mental health issues, addiction, or an inability to find "real connection," without acknowledging the underlying belief systems that perpetuate these cycles. We live in a culture with a vision of toughness and "strength." Many of us want to be invincible.

CHAPTER 7

Vulnerability in Leadership

Furthermore, specifically in the area of team leadership, team leaders who are perceived as being open, human, and transparent may create a greater sense of psychological safety in the culture of their team, wherein team members find the team a safe place to take risks and share their actual feelings without fear of negative consequences to themselves, their image, or their position in the team. While vulnerability or authenticity can be a powerful leadership characteristic, it can be difficult to implement and be tricky to use to get the positive effects hoped for. In saying that, however, many leadership habits or characteristics that are positive are difficult to adopt. So, it should be noted, there are arguments both for and against using vulnerability as a leader. However, the arguments for using it usually outweigh the arguments against it. It naturally follows that it is important to state there are appropriate times to use vulnerability as well, as some would argue bringing emotions into the workplace is a sign of weak leadership.

When discussing vulnerability and its applications, it is important to devote a few lines to vulnerability in leadership. The concept of authenticity as a leadership trait has become increasingly popular over the past few years, especially within the research on authentic leadership. This construct suggests that people can and will follow those leaders who they believe are truly human, who in other words are not perfect. As such, this theory calls for leaders to display their true selves to their followers and, if appropriate, share their fears, dreams, and individual thoughts with them. Vulnerability and authentic leadership share similarities in that they involve a certain degree of openness and transparency usually associated with self-disclosure, in that they show a full spectrum of leadership, and in their consequences as they generate forms of trust and respect that might be otherwise difficult to gain, especially when this image of authenticity includes an impartial caring for those under a leader's responsibility. Along this line of reasoning, authentic leaders are often seen as a source of strength and inspiration to their followers, of course depending upon when and how this authenticity is displayed.

Authentic Leadership Styles

With the changing business environment and increases in complexity and pace, there is the potential for more employee roles to be filled by innovative professionals, known as knowledge-based employees. Organizational cultures can produce innovative products and contribute to the development of new frameworks, providing the organization with a competitive edge. Zaugg et al. (2008) suggest that organizations competing on innovation do so based on bricks and brains—human and social capital. Brains coexist in the realm of knowledge and innovation among these employees. Authentic leaders are likely to attract followers. Indeed, George lays out a typology of leaders based on degrees of self-awareness and self-regulation.

These are the required cornerstones to which authentic leaders are drawn. Authentic leadership likewise enhances relational transparency and fosters trust between those in charge and the audiences. Increasingly, contact with leaders, and their ability to communicate with clarity, honesty, integrity, and credibility, is being sought after. To re-engage in the debate about the relationship between leaders and the led, the matter of leaders and how transparent they ought to be deserves to be revisited. Fully transparent leaders are not likely to be immune from other leaders or colleagues taking advantage of them, but they may command extraordinary psychological power over people who are not decision-makers. The clearer an individual is in respect of values, judgments, and intentions, the more confidence people are likely to have.

Authentic leadership has rapidly become a significantly influential leadership characteristic at the executive level and has been found to have positive effects on employee performance at lower levels of management. Riggio (2008) suggests that authentic leaders are straightforward, open, honest, and act in accordance with their values and place greater emphasis on building authentic relationships with others. Within the workplace, research has shown that leaders who demonstrate authenticity are thought to be more compelling and are more trusted and accepted by their employees. This has led some to develop a trait-based approach which focuses on personal characteristics that distinguish authentic leaders from others. It is hence proposed that the authentic individual is straightforward, honest, possesses integrity, candid, self-aware, genuine, and less focused on costs. Authentic leaders are likely to set aside their own self-interest and place the organization's well-being first. This benchmark is also supported by Duane and Lussier (2011) who avow that authentic leadership can be seen to be a combination of charismatic, transformational, servant, and spiritual leadership. All these styles provide a way for the leader to demonstrate the importance of trust, transparency, and respect for individuals—both of which are the key elements of authentic leadership.

Fostering Psychological Safety in Teams

Instead of enforcing therapeutic change in our communities, we are also advocating that it is probably the humanity behind our professional masks that fosters any respect that is sometimes given to hierarchical leadership. FineGrief, Moga, Zerden, LeBarron, and Englar-Carlson (2009), social work experts seeking to support group work practice, found that students made the link that the team leader's disclosures drew the team together. Furthermore, nearly all of them said that unless they delivered a self-disclosure, they were willing to give them to the class if they were the chief. Therefore, they can begin their work toward exposing the authenticity of their squad members. Although OSLC has collaborated with some teams to build a level of intensity to discuss the challenge, many teams find the initial phase of developing faith to be of profound use. However, it is important not to underestimate the value of photo sharing.

Helping therapists achieve success with EBTs in community-based settings is a complex task. However, a distinguishing feature of higher-performing organizations that implement EBTs is the creation of a culture of psychological safety within their teams. By embracing the power of vulnerability, experts argue that authentic communication, risk-taking, and team cohesion are bolstered. In discussing the importance of psychological safety with implementation teams, OSLC staff frequently hear concerns about a lack of authenticity in their teams. However, this finding is hardly surprising given that all of us doubt the acceptability of revealing the humanity lurking behind our professional masks.

CHAPTER 8

Vulnerability in Creativity and Innovation

Moreover, vulnerability is the root of art and the source of all inspiration. For example, storytelling by its nature can be very vulnerable, at least in a way that storytellers need to allow themselves to be a little bit vulnerable to their audience. Consequently, art is the key to creativity: worth noting, TED speakers admit that applying one's vulnerable feelings can significantly energize and expand creativity. Indeed, renowned creativity researcher Mihaly Csikszentmihalyi found that many of the most creative individuals are willing to face their limitations and are not afraid to be judged on them, which is why deep vulnerability can make enough room for creativity to flourish. Instead of trying not to feel vulnerable, a better strategy may be to throw oneself fully into the experience, vulnerability and all. Vulnerability is the genesis of creativity and the birthplace of innovation and originality.

The concept of vulnerability is broad and connects to every aspect of human existence. Yet vulnerability extends beyond the daily social construct and also informs several other spheres, such as business. As defined by the Oxford dictionary, innovation is the introduction of new things, ideas, or ways of doing something, including creative improvement. Because vulnerability is essentially about courage, one of the dimensions of vulnerability is creativity. Creativity is an act of courage, as creative endeavors, such as creating something that did not exist before, subject an individual to judgment, criticism, and the fear of disconnection. Creatives should fight this fear and take risks in their fields and innovations, as Brené Brown acknowledges, "vulnerability is the birthplace of innovation, creativity, and change".

CHAPTER 9

Vulnerability in Personal Well-being

Vulnerability is strongly connected to compassion toward both one's self and others. Brown (2008) postulates that the ability to embody self-compassion is derived from a willingness to embrace one's vulnerability. Authentic self-compassion is only manifested if individuals epitomize the spirit of vulnerability, the courage of imperfection, and the power to develop new patterns of relating and interacting with themselves. Practicing self-compassion allows individuals to be kind to themselves as they would be with others in moments of deep personal struggle and deserves to be accepted and valued just as others' vulnerabilities and flaws are. Expanding the compassionate energy to transform an individual includes exposing their weaknesses, allowing room to experience transformative growth that is full of possibility.

Renowned speaker and author, Dr. Brené Brown, attributes vulnerability as the foundation to whole-hearted living. She asserts that individuals who exhibit emotional courage are happier, have lower levels of depression and anxiety, and have a higher level of life satisfaction. It is not vulnerability alone that causes individuals to demonstrate higher overall well-being; rather, it is how individuals view vulnerability as it relates to themselves. Fully accepting the highly vulnerable nature of being human is what prepares individuals for the uncertainty of the future and allows them to engage and evolve with life's dynamic nature. It encourages individuals to embrace the entire human experience and dismiss the "false safety of perfectionism" and hiding their true selves.

Embracing Imperfection

Adopting the mindset that we can always do better helps strengthen our capacity for self-compassion and resilience. It's so important to individualism to know that they are, against all odds, okay as they are. Such a belief is during, revolving around the idea of inherent limitations that render us as unacceptable, unworthy of connection and love. The average individual becomes ascriptivist in assessing not only what is and isn't acceptable, but what is and isn't conceivable by and for others, handing down a damning indictment based on purely speculative beliefs to an adoring jury. By divorcing ourselves from our accomplishments and celebrating the value of our actual selves—not what we or others perceive as our accomplishments—we can confront the poisonous aftertaste of our self-imposed "flaws" with grace, self-compassion, and growth. Through such contemplation, individuals can dislodge their damaging inner monologue, cultivating a flexibility to adapt to the ebbs and flows that life throws at our feet.

Before even beginning to embrace the power of vulnerability, it can never hurt to expose the destructive beliefs which manifest under the belief in perfectionism. Flaws, in the context of setting the bar so incredibly high for oneself, can typically be directed as nothing more than a personal insult to one's self. Allowing for self-appraisal helps those who suffer from such unrealistic expectations to decouple themselves from the ideas of conformity, emphasizing the natural individualism in our wonderful tapestry of life. In such, adversity serves as a great teacher, providing us with experiences that can translate to a flint, sharpening our nurturing edge through learning, exploration, and recognition of what really is important in the grand scheme of our lives and to others.

Self-Compassion

Neff found in her research that self-compassion buffers the effects of stress on symptoms of psychological disorders. Furthermore, self-kindness rather than self-criticism has been shown to protect against feelings of isolation and disconnection. Difficulty in being compassionate with oneself is associated with increases in self-loathing, shame, and poor connection with others. All these protect individuals from the risk of achieving high-quality relationships and from attracting prospective partners because it is the way individuals feel about themselves that attract others. Without self-compassion, Brown conjectures, individuals can't forgive themselves for making a mistake, for failing, for being inadequate, or for saying "I'm sorry." Striving for self-compassion is a powerful step toward gaining balance. It requires a more authentic and grounded focus on taking care of yourself rather than an "inflated view of oneself or of denial of one's faults."

A lovingly developed aspect of vulnerability that allows for connection, as opposed to a fault that makes one unworthy of connection, is the capacity for self-compassion, or the act of being kind to oneself. When people begin to accept themselves as they are, with all their imperfections, they become able to connect in more meaningful ways with others. Self-compassion actually appears to create a protective buffer against dehumanization as a result of life's hardships. This is why Brene Brown insists that "pristine perfection is a dragon that 'dehumanizes'." And self-compassion can impact the individual's health. Empirical studies support the conclusion that self-compassion enhances overall well-being.

CHAPTER 10

Cultural Perspectives on Vulnerability

Moving not far from home, the South African "Ubuntu" system of value considers an individual as part of the whole. Social philosophy has Ubuntu as the belief that we are only human through others. In the well-known definition: "Umuntu ngumuntu ngabantu" – "a person is a person through other persons". It is seen as the philosophy of "openness to others" and as having trust in others. So, to be human means to trust others. Vulnerability is an essential quality and perception of the essential self. In "world citizen" psychology perspectives on vulnerability, some reference is made to all cultural perspectives, as one studies the universality of human vulnerability and how disgrace and failure affect us all. There is no hierarchy in vulnerability, and we are all equally entitled to express our vulnerabilities and seek support from others.

From a global perspective, the attitude or response towards being vulnerable, as well as the reason or intention, varies as it is viewed through different cultural lenses. In ancient Eastern philosophies, such as India's tantra yoga, there is a belief that when we lower our guard (i.e. allowing ourselves to be vulnerable), we are in a space to have revelation and experience the divine self, and ultimately find liberation from the material world – where we are only vulnerable to our mortal bodies. Buddhism teaches that courageous vulnerability and engaging with the process of discomfort have been, for many, the very road to enlightenment. In other belief systems such as Christianity and Judaism, vulnerability is seen as trust and having faith in others. The more one recognizes one's status as a child of God, the more one is loved and accepted. And they are reminded that everything is in the hand of God; therefore, being vulnerable and taking risks is seen as part of God's will.

CHAPTER 11

Research and Case Studies on Vulnerability

The point for people undergoing hugely accentuated experience of vulnerability is, oftentimes one may exert a great, and 100% authentic, telling effect on another person or persons undergoing similar situations. In fact, in the right context, the degree of one's lived experience can be directly proportional to the intensity of effect upon an analogous "sufferer." Such powerful stimuli can activate subjective mere-exposure effect, deep empathy, and even a hard-reset of associates' adaptation-level tactics.

The following contains thoughts that are consistently supported by empirical evidence, although the sources cover a range of institutions - such as Harvard, MIT, and the U.S. Military Academy. In a metaphorical way, the heart of today's research is a statement by renowned psychotherapist Irving Yalom, "What is most personal is most universal." Now, let us have a glimpse behind the curtain, with scientific studies and people's true stories. But Kolb extends the notion of "real learning" to include taking wisdom from vulnerability.

How Principally Marginal Individuals Can Wield Acute Influence Both in One-on-One and in Social-Risking Manner.

The field of vulnerability is still very much in progress of being defined. Yet, it is only in exploring depths can we hope to elevate and turn our vulnerabilities into greater strengths.

CHAPTER 12

Conclusion and Call to Action

In the end of Brown's work, readers are left open to the possibility that work still remains to be done, particularly by dedicating oneself to developing resilience. Having embraced the possibility of failure that vulnerability opens through resilience, perhaps readers will be inclined to take up Brown's call to join the movement—an interpersonal historical event of embracing vulnerability that is revolutionizing how we think. Brown shows that by reconnecting to this long-lost humanity, we have an opportunity to alter social worlds that are marked by a generally rooted sense of scarcity and lack into social worlds where we feel and own our value jointly. She challenges us to join a movement of living authentically. Through this, we can create changes in society to rise above exploitative competition as we count one another to be ours and the world's best hope. What all of us must do is have the courage to show our genuine selves and to not back down when we come up against those who would diminish the value of vulnerability at all, whether they are inside or outside of our own heads. Together, we can and will bring forth the world we wish to bequest to future generations.

Living wholeheartedly means embracing both the good and the bad, and having the courage to live an authentic and open life. According to Brown, the true power of vulnerability is recognition of the fact that failure can lead to success, loss can lead to gains, and people across the world share the bond of humanity. With this in mind, we can realize that although we may feel undeserving of our share, possessing human qualities such as love, connection, and belief are states of being. They are birthrights, not prizes we pick up for esteemed individual accomplishment or roles played in life. In order to take advantage of the power of vulnerability, it is necessary to recognize and nurture the things that can't be taken away.